MOZART

COMPLETE MUSIC FOR PIANO 4 HANDS

3036

Due to the length of the original recordings
no repeats or first endings were taken.
Please mark your score accordingly.

SONATA I.

W. A. Mozart.

Allegro. 4 taps precede music.

PRIMO.

Andante. 3 taps precede music

sotto voce

legato

più f

B1

p

cresc.

p dolce

f

p

Allegro molto. 2 taps precede music.

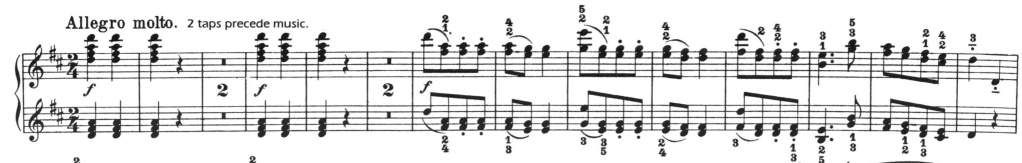

Due to the length of the original recordings
no repeats or first endings were taken.
Please mark your score accordingly.

SONATA II.

Adagio. 3 taps precede music.

2 taps precede Molto presto.
music.

SONATA III.

Due to the length of the original recordings
no repeats or first endings were taken.
Please mark your score accordingly.

3 taps precede music.

4 taps precede music.

2 taps precede music.

Due to the length of the original recordings
no repeats or first endings were taken.
Please mark your score accordingly.

SONATA IV.

4 taps precede music.

Allegro.

PRIMO.

3 taps precede music

Andante.

A

p dolce

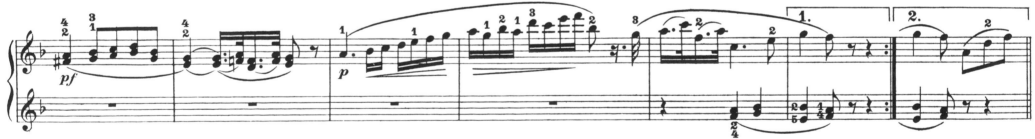

Allegretto. 2 taps precede music.

FANTASIA I.

Due to the length of the original recordings
no repeats or first endings were taken.
Please mark your score accordingly.

Adagio.   3 taps precede music.

Allegro

FANTASIA II.

TEMA CON VARIAZIONI.

Var. III.

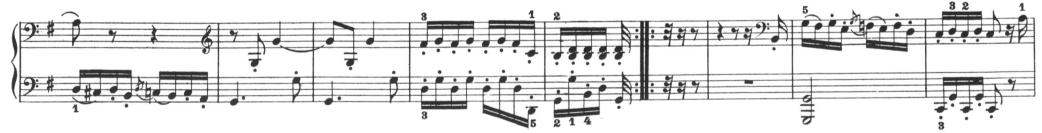

FUGA.

MUSIC MINUS ONE 50 Executive Boulevard • Elmsford New York 10523-1325